Grown-ups play games, too.

People play games for fun.

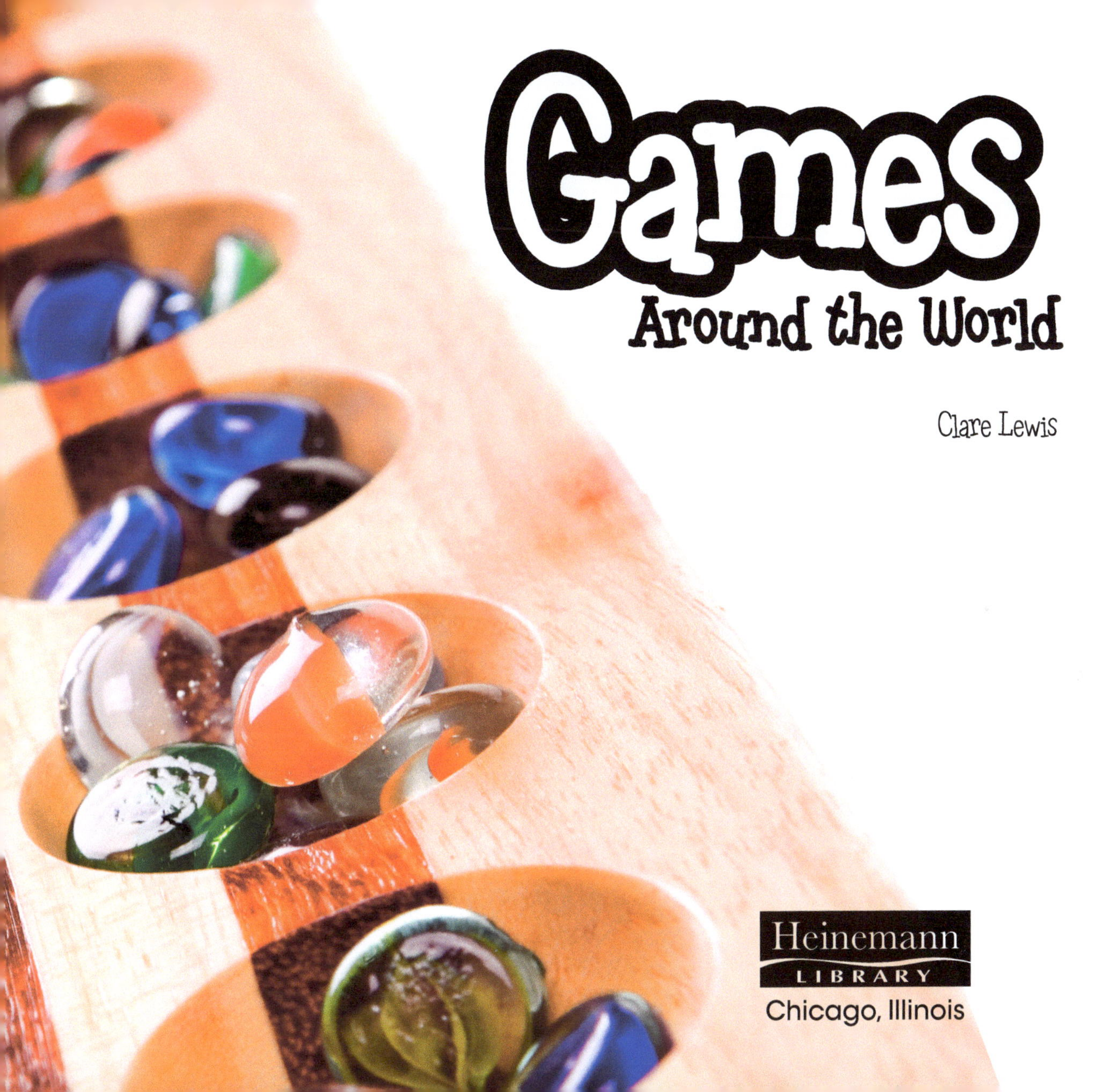

Games

Around the World

Clare Lewis

Heinemann
LIBRARY

Chicago, Illinois

Edited by Joanna Issa, Shelly Lyons, Diyan Leake, and Helen Cox Cannons
Designed by Cynthia Akiyoshi
Original illustrations © Capstone Global Library Ltd 2014
Picture research by Elizabeth Alexander and Tracy Cummins
Production by Victoria Fitzgerald
Originated by Capstone Global Library Ltd

Library of Congress Cataloging-in-Publication Data
Lewis, Clare.
  Games around the world / Clare Lewis.
    pages cm.—(Around the world)
  Includes bibliographical references and index.
  ISBN 978-1-4846-0371-0 (hb)—ISBN 978-1-4846-0378-9 (pb) 1. Games—Juvenile literature. 2. Games—Cross-cultural studies—Juvenile literature. I. Title.

GV1203.L473 2015
790.1—dc23   2013040506

Image Credits
Almay: AHOWDEN INTERNATIONAL, 8, 22 (bottom right), David Litschel, 16, Greatstock, 13, 22 (bottom middle), Neil McAllister, 15, 23 (top), Patrick Eden, 4, Peter Horree, 12, 22 (bottom left), View Stock, 6; Getty Images: David Patrick Valera, 10, Fabrice LEROUGE, 18, FG Trade Latin, 17, JGI/Jamie Grill, 20, Manfred Gottschalk, 5, 22 (top left), poco_bw, cover, Tim Hall, 21; Shutterstock: 2happy, 1, Africa Studio, 24 (soccer ball), Dan Kosmayer, 24 (marble), effe45, 2, Jacek Chabraszewski, 11, 23 (bottom), Kirk Peart Professional Imaging, 7, Olga Popova, 24 (beach ball), pio3, 3, RTimages, 24 (cricket ball), STILLFX, 24 (stone), Tomislav Forgo, 24 (baseball); SuperStock: Chevalier Virginie/Oredia Eurl, 14, back cover, PhotoAlto, 9, Travel Library Limited, 19, 22 (top right)

Every effort has been made to contact copyright holders of material reproduced in this book. Any omissions will
be rectified in subsequent printings if notice is given to the publisher.

All the Internet addresses (URLs) given in this book were valid at the time of going to press. However, due to the dynamic nature of the Internet, some addresses may have changed, or sites may have changed or ceased to exist since publication. While the author and publisher regret any inconvenience this may cause readers, no responsibility for any such changes can be accepted by either the author or the publisher.

Contents

Games Everywhere

All around the world, children play games.

Sometimes people watch other people play games.

Games with Friends

People play games with their friends.

Friends can play games with pens and paper.

Games Alone

People play games alone.

People play games on screens.

Different Types of Games

People play ball games.

People play soccer.

People play card games.

People play board games.

People play skipping games.

People play clapping games.

People play games with sticks.

People play games with stones.

People play make-believe games.

What games do you like to play?

Map of Games Around the World

Picture Glossary

board game game that has pieces that are moved along a board

screen part of a computer or tablet that you look at to see the pictures or writing

Index

Notes for parents and teachers

Before reading

Read the title of the book and then write the word *games* on the board. Ask children to name some games they know about, recording their answers as a list. Turn to page 24 of the book and explain that the index is a tool that helps readers find specific information in a book. Read the index entries and notice if there are any items that are similar to the list on the board. Demonstrate how to use the index to find the page where that type of game is mentioned.

After reading

- Review the list made before reading the book. Ask children if they learned about any other types of game from reading the book. Add them to the list.

- Turn to the map on page 22 and identify the seven continents with children. Discuss how this book is about games that are played all over the world, and demonstrate how this map is a tool that identifies where some of the photos were taken.

- Discuss that games often have rules that players must follow. Have children identify a familiar game (such as a game played at recess) and make a list of rules that they follow when they play the game. Depending on the age and ability of the children, you might have them work in pairs, or it could be a whole class activity.